HAL•LEONARD
INSTRUMENTAL
PLAY-ALONG

AUDIO
ACCESS
INCLUDED

PLAYBACK+
Speed • Pitch • Balance • Loop

TROMBONE

DIXIELAND Favorites

Audio arrangements by Peter Deneff

To access audio visit:
www.halleonard.com/mylibrary

4367-9917-2261-3821

ISBN 978-1-5400-2432-9

HAL•LEONARD®
7777 W. BLUEMOUND RD. P.O. BOX 13819 MILWAUKEE, WI 53213

Visit Hal Leonard Online at
www.halleonard.com

BASIN STREET BLUES

TROMBONE

Words and Music by
SPENCER WILLIAMS

BILL BAILEY,
WON'T YOU PLEASE COME HOME

TROMBONE

Words and Music by
HUGHIE CANNON

BLACK BOTTOM STOMP

TROMBONE

By FERD "Jelly Roll" MORTON

BUGLE CALL RAG

TROMBONE

By HUBERT BLAKE
and CAREY MORGAN

COPENHAGEN

TROMBONE

Lyric by WALTER MELROSE
Music by CHARLIE DAVIS

HIGH SOCIETY

TROMBONE

By PORTER STEELE
and WALTER MELROSE

(small notes optional)

MAPLE LEAF RAG

TROMBONE

Music by SCOTT JOPLIN

MUSKRAT RAMBLE

TROMBONE

Written by EDWARD ORY
and RAY GILBERT

ROYAL GARDEN BLUES

TROMBONE

Words and Music by CLARENCE WILLIAMS
and SPENCER WILLIAMS

SOUTH RAMPART STREET PARADE

Words by STEVE ALLEN
Music by RAY BAUDUC and BOB HAGGART

TROMBONE

SWEET GEORGIA BROWN

TROMBONE

Words and Music by BEN BERNIE,
MACEO PINKARD and KENNETH CASEY

TIGER RAG
(Hold That Tiger)

Words by HARRY DeCOSTA
Music by Original Dixieland Jazz Band

TROMBONE

TIN ROOF BLUES

TROMBONE

Lyric by WALTER MELROSE
Music by New Orleans Rhythm Kings

'WAY DOWN YONDER IN NEW ORLEANS

TROMBONE

Words and Music by HENRY CREAMER
and J. TURNER LAYTON

WHEN THE SAINTS GO MARCHING IN

TROMBONE

Words by KATHERINE E. PURVIS
Music by JAMES M. BLACK

HAL•LEONARD INSTRUMENTAL PLAY-ALONG

Your favorite songs are arranged just for solo instrumentalists with this outstanding series. Each book includes a great full-accompaniment play-along audio so you can sound just like a pro! Check out **www.halleonard.com** to see all the titles available.

The Beatles

All You Need Is Love • Blackbird • Day Tripper • Eleanor Rigby • Get Back • Here, There and Everywhere • Hey Jude • I Will • Let It Be • Lucy in the Sky with Diamonds • Ob-La-Di, Ob-La-Da • Penny Lane • Something • Ticket to Ride • Yesterday.

00225330	Flute	$14.99
00225331	Clarinet	$14.99
00225332	Alto Sax	$14.99
00225333	Tenor Sax	$14.99
00225334	Trumpet	$14.99
00225335	Horn	$14.99
00225336	Trombone	$14.99
00225337	Violin	$14.99
00225338	Viola	$14.99
00225339	Cello	$14.99

Chart Hits

All About That Bass • All of Me • Happy • Radioactive • Roar • Say Something • Shake It Off • A Sky Full of Stars • Someone like You • Stay with Me • Thinking Out Loud • Uptown Funk.

00146207	Flute	$12.99
00146208	Clarinet	$12.99
00146209	Alto Sax	$12.99
00146210	Tenor Sax	$12.99
00146211	Trumpet	$12.99
00146212	Horn	$12.99
00146213	Trombone	$12.99
00146214	Violin	$12.99
00146215	Viola	$12.99
00146216	Cello	$12.99

Coldplay

Clocks • Every Teardrop Is a Waterfall • Fix You • In My Place • Lost! • Paradise • The Scientist • Speed of Sound • Trouble • Violet Hill • Viva La Vida • Yellow.

00103337	Flute	$12.99
00103338	Clarinet	$12.99
00103339	Alto Sax	$12.99
00103340	Tenor Sax	$12.99
00103341	Trumpet	$12.99
00103342	Horn	$12.99
00103343	Trombone	$12.99
00103344	Violin	$12.99
00103345	Viola	$12.99
00103346	Cello	$12.99

Disney Greats

Arabian Nights • Hawaiian Roller Coaster Ride • It's a Small World • Look Through My Eyes • Yo Ho (A Pirate's Life for Me) • and more.

00841934	Flute	$12.99
00841935	Clarinet	$12.99
00841936	Alto Sax	$12.99
00841937	Tenor Sax	$12.95
00841938	Trumpet	$12.99
00841939	Horn	$12.99
00841940	Trombone	$12.99
00841941	Violin	$12.99
00841942	Viola	$12.99
00841943	Cello	$12.99
00842078	Oboe	$12.99

Great Themes

Bella's Lullaby • Chariots of Fire • Get Smart • Hawaii Five-O Theme • I Love Lucy • The Odd Couple • Spanish Flea • and more.

00842468	Flute	$12.99
00842469	Clarinet	$12.99
00842470	Alto Sax	$12.99
00842471	Tenor Sax	$12.99
00842472	Trumpet	$12.99
00842473	Horn	$12.99
00842474	Trombone	$12.99
00842475	Violin	$12.99
00842476	Viola	$12.99
00842477	Cello	$12.99

Popular Hits

Breakeven • Fireflies • Halo • Hey, Soul Sister • I Gotta Feeling • I'm Yours • Need You Now • Poker Face • Viva La Vida • You Belong with Me • and more.

00842511	Flute	$12.99
00842512	Clarinet	$12.99
00842513	Alto Sax	$12.99
00842514	Tenor Sax	$12.99
00842515	Trumpet	$12.99
00842516	Horn	$12.99
00842517	Trombone	$12.99
00842518	Violin	$12.99
00842519	Viola	$12.99
00842520	Cello	$12.99

Songs from Frozen, Tangled and Enchanted

Do You Want to Build a Snowman? • For the First Time in Forever • Happy Working Song • I See the Light • In Summer • Let It Go • Mother Knows Best • That's How You Know • True Love's First Kiss • When Will My Life Begin • and more.

00126921	Flute	$14.99
00126922	Clarinet	$14.99
00126923	Alto Sax	$14.99
00126924	Tenor Sax	$14.99
00126925	Trumpet	$14.99
00126926	Horn	$14.99
00126927	Trombone	$14.99
00126928	Violin	$14.99
00126929	Viola	$14.99
00126930	Cello	$14.99

Top Hits

Adventure of a Lifetime • Budapest • Die a Happy Man • Ex's & Oh's • Fight Song • Hello • Let It Go • Love Yourself • One Call Away • Pillowtalk • Stitches • Writing's on the Wall.

00171073	Flute	$12.99
00171074	Clarinet	$12.99
00171075	Alto Sax	$12.99
00171106	Tenor Sax	$12.99
00171107	Trumpet	$12.99
00171108	Horn	$12.99
00171109	Trombone	$12.99
00171110	Violin	$12.99
00171111	Viola	$12.99
00171112	Cello	$12.99

Wicked

As Long As You're Mine • Dancing Through Life • Defying Gravity • For Good • I'm Not That Girl • Popular • The Wizard and I • and more.

00842236	Flute	$12.99
00842237	Clarinet	$12.99
00842238	Alto Saxophone	$11.95
00842239	Tenor Saxophone	$11.95
00842240	Trumpet	$11.99
00842241	Horn	$12.99
00842242	Trombone	$12.99
00842243	Violin	$11.99
00842244	Viola	$12.99
00842245	Cello	$12.99

HAL•LEONARD®